Why Me?

Boys are molested too

CT Kirk

authorHOUSE®

AuthorHouse™
1663 Liberty Drive
Bloomington, IN 47403
www.authorhouse.com
Phone: 833-262-8899

Published by AuthorHouse 07/07/2022

Library of Congress Control Number: 2022912481

ISBN: 978-1-6655-6426-7 (sc)
ISBN: 978-1-6655-6425-0 (e)

Print information available on the last page.

Contents

Dedication

This book is dedicated to my wife, Monique, and our three children: Anela, Brendan, and Kyndall.

To my parents for having the courage to allow me to share my story even though it came with great pain and hurt.

To the Sanctuary of Life Outreach Center Family for supporting me as your pastor and brother in Christ.

To my brothers and friends, Walter "Walt Tee" White, Royal Blake, Gilbert Burgess, and Terrance Culp for helping me see the importance of this work. Your advice and prayers helped me push through the difficult moments to finish this assignment.

To Dr. Kimberly Johnson motivating me to write. You helped me find my voice, and I will always be grateful.

To all of the silent heroes that suffered in secret but now have the courage to tell their stories.

Note:

The biggest difference between molestation and sexual abuse is the age of the victim. Molestation is seen commonly with children, but sexual abuse can occur at any age. At times during this writing, both may be referenced in order to cover men at any age of their offense. (RAINN, 2021)

Legal definition of molestation (Nolo's Plain-English Law Dictionary):

The crime of sexual acts with children up to the age of 18, including touching of private parts, exposure of genitalia, taking of pornographic pictures, rape, inducement of sexual acts with the molester or with other children, and variations of these acts.

Disclaimer:

I am not a clinical psychologist or psychiatrist, and I do not have a degree in these areas of study, but I know what it is like to be a victim of sexual abuse.

This work is a non-fiction work. The characters in the book are unnamed but real people.

Chapter One

The Taboo Topic

Why is molestation among boys a taboo topic? Sorry to start the book with a question, but when was the last time you heard of a male sharing their story of being molested? Unbeknownst to me, I did it again. I asked a question as though I would be around to hear you give me an answer. Quite frankly, molestation amidst boys is a topic rarely discussed in our society. A man can walk into a barbershop his whole life and never hear the topic of molestation amidst children mentioned unless someone famous is involved in the situation. There are few movies or television shows tailor-made to approach the topic of molestation or sexual abuse when it comes to males. I have been to quite a few religious male conferences, workshops, seminars, and small groups, and I cannot recall one topic surrounding men being molested.

According to a 2005 report from the Center for Disease Control, one in five males have been sexually assaulted or molested under the age of 18. In 2015, the Center for Disease Control and Prevention found that over 2 million men had been victims of some type of sexual abuse. It is also reported that this is an estimation being that only 16% of males will come forward with their cases of molestation. Whereas 84% of women will come forward with either being raped or molested or sexually assaulted. Why are men so afraid to come forward with their stories? Is it the fear of being judged? Is it shame or embarrassment?

Or could it be that our society is not formed where a man can feel comfortable coming forth with his story of molestation?

According to the 1in6 website, there are many myths that surround molestation amidst boys. Let's deal with four of these myths:

1. *The myth that most men who sexually abused boys are gay.* According to many studies, most males that sexually assault other males consider themselves as heterosexual (straight). The 1in6 website suggests that the sexual orientation of the abusive person is not really relevant to an abusive interaction. A closer look reveals that sexual abuse or molestation is not a sexual relationship but it is an assault. There is really no simple reason a person may misuse their position, their power, or their influence to sexually assault a child. The answers are very different depending on the person which often creates a very complex scenario. Studies have shown that the reasons people have sexually assaulted children are due to sexual fantasies, dominance or control of the victim, and past trauma they experienced.

In talking with different male victims of molestation, I noticed that none of these males were molested by homosexual men. In fact, on several occasions, the molester was married to a female or considered to be very masculine. For those men that were molested by a family member, all of the cases ended up with the molester living a life as a heterosexual man. So how is it that a heterosexual male could commit such an act and yet live a heterosexual lifestyle afterwards? According to several studies, heterosexual men that are the molester feel that unless they are the victims of the act, they can resort to their sexuality of choice. Which makes the act of molestation more about dominance and control than the sexual pleasing from the offense.

2. *The myth that victims of molestation or sexual assault will choose a homosexual lifestyle.* According to the article "Myths and Facts about Sexual Abuse and Assault," experts believe sexual orientation is not a direct result of sexual abuse or premature sexual experiences. There is no good evidence that someone can make another person homosexual or heterosexual.

Now this is not to state that boys and young men, who have been abused, do not express some level of confusion about their sexual identity and orientation. In fact, many studies suggest that men have often contemplated whether or not they were homosexual or heterosexual based on their sexual abuse. Even with most cases of males being molested the majority are heterosexual; however, they fear that many men who know their story will consider them as homosexual based on their experiences. Could this be one of the reasons why most males do not speak on their experiences out of fear of being labeled?

No man wants to be identified as homosexual when that it is not the lifestyle he chose. So, many men will keep the hurt and the pain on the inside in order to forget the situation, or battle it in secret. In preparation for this book, I sat down with several survivors of molestation (yes, men are survivors too). For many of them, the hardness of their rearing made it difficult for them to share their stories with family or friends. In the eras before this Modern Era of openness, these men felt that their stories would be used against them. So, instead of being open, many felt that in order to hide it, they needed to show masculinity, even to the point of creating homophobia.

The one common factor that I have experienced as a spiritual counselor is most men have a little boy trapped on the inside of them. (This revelation came to me from the movie *Antwone Fisher*). In this movie, Denzel Washington played a Navy counselor helping a young Navy seaman deal with his past hurts from being raised by a cruel foster mom. The young seaman was also the victim of child molestation at the hands of his foster sister. The little boy represents the part of the man that never fully developed due to a traumatic experience in their life. Suppose a man was molested at the age of 10, chances are this man will still feel the effects of what happened to him years later. In fact, most scientific studies on trauma suggest that the age of the trauma causes the resulting actions years later. Even though many of us look like successful, strong men, a lot of us are still dealing with the brokenness of that little boy on the inside. Imagine, if you will, being broken at such a young age and not having the confidence to tell anyone. So what happens? The man suffers in secret and learns how to be fake in public. The little boy on the inside of him never probably heals, and so the battle for the man becomes proving his sexuality, which can produce perversion, womanizing, broken relationships, and marital issues.

3. *The myth that if a male is abused by a woman he is lucky and really not abused.*

This myth is really ingrained in the mythological world of male masculinity. Let's be honest most men have fantasies about the teacher or older woman engaging them in some sort of sexual manner. Any man that has ever engaged with pornographic materials will tell you that the greatest pleasure of pornographic material is the fantasies it creates. It is not a mystery that a male being sexually abused by a female perpetrator is not as alarming as a male-to-male encounter. In fact, in some cases the female is still seen as a victim of circumstances. Think back on the female teachers that received only probation for sleeping with their male students; and how these females were the victims because of the mistreatment from their husbands or the need to feel loved. Society paints a different picture when a male is molested by a female.

In 2014, Lara Stemple, the director of UCLA's Health and Human Rights Law Project, came across some statistics that blow the lid off of the definition of rape and sexual assault. Stemple discovered that 38% of males have been sexually assaulted by females.

"For years, the FBI defined rape as gendered, requiring "carnal knowledge of a female forcibly and against her will" (The Atlantic, 2016).

I want to be very transparent in this book because I feel someone will read it and connect to each line. As I started to share my story, I was approached by many men with narratives of being molested. I can recall a gentleman that was molested by his older sister's friend telling me his story. Not being mature in my counseling at this point, my first reaction was, "really dude?" Understand at that point, I had only heard from men being molested by men. It was new ground for me to hear that a female molested a man. What I did not realize; until I saw the tears fall from his eyes was that molestation carries the same pain no matter who or what the perpetrator is. Molestation or sexual abuse is not an invitation that can be accepted or rejected, so when a person is made to do something against their will the feeling of defeat and shame is the same. The hidden truth to the molestation or sexual abuse is that it is more than a sexual act, but mental exploitation and betrayal. It takes the innocence away from the person and returns it with a defiled, polluted sense of self.

Surprisingly, the men that experienced molestation from females did not see themselves as more masculine. They were not proud nor did they feel lucky that the offense happened to them. There was no badge of honor to say that they lost their virginity at the age of eight or ten years old. These men saw themselves as I saw myself, a victim of someone else's vile, debauched, deplorable, and perverted mind. These men wrestled with the same fears and painful thoughts of the little boy trapped on the inside crying but no one there to hold him. The night sweats that come with the dreams of being taken advantage of; and the loneliness that comes with having a secret no one can know.

"In reality, premature, coerced, or otherwise abusive or exploitative sexual experiences are never positive – whether they are imposed by an older sister, sister of a friend, babysitter, neighbor, aunt, mother, or any other female in a position of power over a boy. At a minimum, they cause confusion and insecurity. They almost always harm boys' and men's capacities for trust and intimacy," (1in6, 2021).

4. *The myth that molestation or sexual abuse is less harmful to boys than girls.*

There is no denying the fact that women are more likely to be sexually abused. However, what is untrue is that women are the only ones that suffer emotionally from the abuse. In a society where men are built to be tough and unresponsive to feelings, many men that have been molested find themselves sheltering their feelings from the public. The public does not want to hear the story of a man crying over years of hurt and pain is how many men view their struggles.

Before Chronic Traumatic Encephalopathy (CTE) was discovered in football, when a person had symptoms of what we now know as concussions, it was referred to as he got his bell rung. Getting your bell rung was a nice way to say you got popped, and next time be more cautious. I remember at the age of 13, fielding a kickoff at practice. I avoided the first couple of defenders that tried to tackle me. As I spun from one of the defenders, I was blindsided by one of my teammates. The hit was so hard, I was dizzy and confused, and my helmet was backwards. It felt like a train had hit me, and I could hear a whistling in my head. As I laid on the ground, I could hear my teammates laughing and my coaches telling me to get up.

Not to be outshined, I quickly jumped up to show my team I wasn't hurt. I knew that if I complained about the headache or dizziness, I would be ridiculed. I finished the next hour of practice with one of the worst headaches of my life.

As men, many of us are not taught how to be emotional from other men. You either take on the emotions of your mother, another female, or hide your emotions altogether." I was one of those men that learned "The Art of Hiding" because I didn't want to associate myself with anything that made me seem feminine. "The Art of Hiding" is simply my way of not dealing with emotions rather than just having an "I don't care" philosophy. So for years, I did not cry or show a strong sense of emotional fortitude. On the surface, I looked to be an extrovert and life of the party, but inwardly I was an introvert and emotional recluse. It was easier to be fake for the enjoyment of people and then retreat to my room of silence. I'm sure there are plenty of men who feel as though society only cares about you as long as you are performing.

"Boys and men who survive sexual abuse can experience serious psychological and emotional fallout, including post-traumatic stress, symptoms of depression and anxiety, suicidal thoughts, substance abuse problems, and sexual dysfunction," (RAINN, 2021). What's alarming is many of these males will have these struggles and the source of it is never revealed. To all the ladies reading this book, can you imagine being in a relationship with a man hurting and afraid to reveal why? Can you think about it? Many of the same symptoms exist in men that have been emotionally withdrawn, in prison, or addicted to drugs." The same symptoms quoted by Emma Brown are the same symptoms we see in women. Wow. Did you check that? Regardless of gender, pain and hurt from sexual abuse are the same. The main question now is- "Why isn't it viewed as being the same?" Let us be transparent and honest, sexual abuse amidst men does not get the same sorrowful feeling as it does amidst women. In 2016, former NFL player and an accomplished actor came forward to admit being groped by a Hollywood executive at a party. Even though his admission made the headlines, many successful men mocked him because of his outward appearance. For those of you who do not know he stands at 6'2 and around 245 pounds of muscle. On-site, most men would run if he was to get angry. However, in a moment that opened the door for conversation among men and being sexually assaulted or molested, some celebrities made light of the situation. It seems like whenever there has been a case of molestation or sexual assault in the world of the rich and famous, the cases get quietly settled out of court and the media attention quickly goes away.

What if his confession had opened up a nationwide discussion on boys being molested or men being sexually assaulted? Could this open discussion allow more boys and men to come out of hiding and tell their stories? Could this coming out help these boys and men get the support needed to combat past emotional hurts? Instead of this revolution, many of those without the experience mocked he for not beating up the man that groped him. As though a physical battle comforts the war within. This example goes a long way in what society sees as the role of a man. This stigma of "toughness" creates a wall of emotionless men that are afraid to express themselves fully.

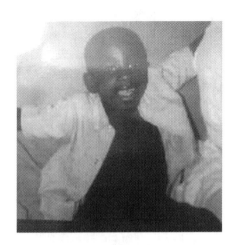

Chapter Two

Boys Are Molested Too

This part of the book has to come first in order to set the mood of my story. I tried for years to drown out this part of my life in order to take away the sting of having to recall the events of that day that changed my life. No matter how much I have accomplished in my life, I still see this moment in my life as a changing point or like a train being derailed from the track. The fact that I can type with tears in my eyes is evident that the pain is still fresh in my brain. In my early 40s, I still feel like that little six-year-old that was innocently taking advantage of and for no reason.

The day in 1986 was a typical day. I remember the command by my grandfather to go outside and play. In the 1980s, it was customary for a child to spend the majority of the day playing in the neighborhood. As always the kids of the neighborhood were like having extended family. These kids taught you just as many life lessons as your parents in some cases. You learned how to invent games, the technique of fighting or fleeing, how to steal from the neighborhood store, how to kiss, and other things that kids of today should never know. My neighborhood was one of poverty in some regards, however, because no one had more than the other we did not see poverty. In fact, outside of the four blocks that made up my neighborhood, we thought everyone lived the same way.

I remember walking to my neighbor's house to play with my best friends, but to my surprise, they were away. After several minutes of wandering aimlessly around in the front yard, I was called to a nearby house by a group of boys from the neighborhood. The boys were older than me by quite a few years, but seeing the brother of one of my close friends gave me relief that the situation wasn't toxic and being six years old it's not like I could discern any red flags. The four boys in their early teens invited me into the house stating that they wanted to play. After several minutes of watching them make fun of each other and play fight, I decided to leave. That's when the older of the four and one that I presumed to be the leader of the group asked if I wanted to play a game.

"If you want to be our friend, you have to agree to play this game with us," he said.

As I reflect on this moment. I understand now that my wanting to be accepted derived from years of dealing with low self-esteem at an early age. Even at six years old, I heard the hurtful words that came with being very dark-skinned, such as being called "Tar Baby" or told I couldn't be seen once the lights were turned off, which caused me to doubt the importance of my existence. Also, understand that in the 80s, there was not a lot of positive reinforcement like we have in the 21st century. You were more likely to get bullied than for someone to say how nice and smart you were. Also, remember that during this time ugly was ugly according to what was defined as beauty by the media, and nowhere during this time was the beauty in being dark-skinned displayed. I say now in humor on many occasions that had Wesley Snipes came along with his hand in the movie *Waiting to Exhale* earlier, my life would have been better. In all accounts, my home life was very loving and pleasant, however, being grabbed for a long hug or words to build up self-esteem was not common. So, of course, any attempt to make friends or to be accepted into a group would be appreciated. This teenager was not as familiar to me, I knew of his younger siblings from school, but had only seen him in passing only one or two times.

Thinking of that moment now, I should have sensed the evil demeanor coming through his sly grin. The very way he carried himself at that moment continues to give me the chills, as I realize the impending danger the six-year-old child was in. I wish for many opportunities to go back to that moment and save myself from the dangers that this evil-guided and immature teenager had in his mind. I can see with perfect vision, the six-year-old boy standing there without a caution sign or warning for the events that so drastically pulled him into a situation of despair, depression, and rout. Maybe if my self-esteem would have been stronger, I wouldn't have longed for acceptance. I know this is a lot to ask of a six-year-old, but maybe this thought process will save other children from feeling they have to be accepted in order to function properly. Maybe this line of rational thinking out loud will help a parent build up the self-esteem in their child.

With the question before me, I quickly accepted the opportunity for friendship. In order to play this game, I was told that I had to go into the bedroom of one of the teenagers who stood by reluctantly, partaking in the suggestion made by the other teenager. The disinclined teen was one that I had known the majority of my life. His brother was a close friend of mine, and I somewhat saw him as my brother. His physique at this moment was nowhere near as cocky as the other teen (I will refer to him as the cocky teen throughout this chapter). In fact, none of the three boys were brash or what I would call willing participants in the thought process of the other teen. However, like many boys of that day, it was easier to go along with the plan than to stand up and be considered a recluse. As I was led into the bedroom, I had no reason to feel fear or restraints. I thought this would be another attempt to wrestle as or play around as many times as possible. Understand the chills that are coming over me as I attempt to write down the next events that shake me to my core. I will try to lessen the intensity of this portion of the story for the sake of political correctness. The room was one of low-income living with just a bed, bare with no sheets, comforter, just the white mattress, and a dresser that was surely secondhand. The atmosphere was sad as only a light shining through the window emulated the dreary, gloomy feeling in the room. No wall decorations, cheap white paint on the walls filled with dirt marks and dirty fingerprints, however, it appeared to be more of an adult's room or an older sibling because it showed signs that whoever rested there tried their best to make it suitable in spite of their financial shortages.

The cocky teen grabbed my buttocks as though he was committing the lewd act upon an unexpected female. "He has a tiny, little, hard butt", he said to the others. He motioned for them to grab as well to prove his theory. The others slowly took turns, as their hesitancy was quite apparent. His next actions were to belittle any ounce of innocence that I had in my six-year-old body, as he commanded my hands first on his buttocks then over other parts of my body. He proceeded to make sure this action was repetitive on the others so that he would not look like the only guilty party in this hideous act. His vulgar and humiliating act only intensified his passion. He thrusted on top of me, kissing me as though I was a teenage girl. How could my first kiss, outside of the peck on the cheek I gave my mother before bed, be with a person of the same sex? Not only did I not know about kissing, but the mere sight of kissing a boy also was not something that I wanted or invited. Yet, I find myself in the mercies of a teenage boy while others are surrounded laughing. Every action that he attempted, he made sure that the others followed his lead. However, at this moment the acts had to be either so perverted or they felt pity for me that they never fully acted them out. For example, instead of kissing me they simply laid on me and mimicked the act. The cocky teenager was too much engulfed in laughter and sinister thinking to notice that the others were not fully engaged in the process. Even though I do not see them in any positive regard for not stopping him; the fact they had a little ounce of decency not to continue these degrading and malicious acts somewhat saved me from the obvious plans of the cocky teen.

As I prepare myself mentally to go forward, I must warn you that this next part of this story took over 30 years to be able to talk about in detail. Understand I have only told portions of this story and never this part because it reminds me of the rage of having to relive the moment. I warn you now that this portion of the story is both graphic and insulting for me to tell. In fact, the bravery to tell this portion is to get you to understand that molestation is real in a lot of the stories of men today. So many men are afraid to tell their stories out of the pain and humiliation it causes to relive it. In fact, I will tell you that no matter how old an offense maybe--- the pain is still there. So, I hope that telling my story will give others the ability to speak their truths, in order for the healing process to begin.

The cocky teenager proceeded to make me perform sexual acts on him. In order to ensure he would get the most pleasurable experience possible, he had me practice by putting his finger in my mouth. If at any time he felt the slightest scrape of my teeth on his finger, he slapped me upside my head. I remember the third blow being so hard that it caused me to cry. Understanding the key to any abuse is 30 percent physical and 70 percent mental. So to subject my crying to both being hit and being choked by his finger in my mouth; I was told repeatedly that if I kept crying I would get in trouble because there were four of them and only one of me. He also assured me that if I kept crying he would hit me again. So, I knew that continuing to cry would only result in more punishment. I also knew that I had no help and the reluctant teenagers would only be bystanders to the abuse. His next actions were to remove his finger and replace it with his private part, reminding me that if he felt one tooth he would punch me in my face. At this point, I am pinned down on the bed. His knees are on my shoulders and my mobility is limited. With the thought of this excruciating memory, I find myself stopping several times and walking away from the computer with tears in my eyes. Amazingly, 30 plus years later, I still have the fear of that day crippling my ability to type.

I walk to the computer, type a few lines, and then quickly walk away breathing hard. I know that I must finish this chapter, but the shame and hurt is so much for me to handle at times. I know now why women who have been raped carry those fears of that moment around so heavy in their lives. Once the physical hurts heal, you are forced to contend with those emotional scars that are constant reminders of the pain you suffered. I can still hear his voice echoing the consequences if he felt a tooth. His fist balled up and in position to strike at any moment. The sounds of the smirks coming from the other boys. After his moments of pleasure, he motioned for the next boy to come and be a part of his despicable act. I cry for that six-year-old boy as though it was not me but a helpless child that I am watching from afar. The adult me wants to save the young me and the helplessness is surreal.

One by one the other teens would pin me down like they witnessed the cocky teen had. The only exception was that inside, forcing me to perform orally on them, they placed their fingers through their zippers so that it appeared like it was their private parts. It's crazy that three followers would all have the same mind frame to not fully engulf themselves in the behavior of the cocky teen. I often wonder if it was mercy for me or if the thoughts of committing such a repulsive act was too much for their conscience to ingest. Whatever the case was, it caused me not to remember their faces, only the cocky teenager and the one I knew my whole life. After their rounds, the cocky teenager was not finished with me. He climbed back on top of me in the manner in which he had previously done. Once again he barked the same orders as before and committed to doing the same act as before. To add further insult, he tells me to kiss his buttocks as a sign of assertive power at that moment.

Apparently, that's when the other teens had enough of his twisted game and convinced him to stop. Surely, had they not stopped this cocky teenager he would have gone further as he insisted that I needed to remove my clothing. I would never glamourize them as heroes, but I do understand that whatever caused them to stop surely saved my innocence from being further stripped. No telling what could have happened to me had not the interference occurred, and even though it has been painful for you to read this much, I can only envision what could have been the rest of the story.

I remember getting up from the bed and saying to the teens, "I'm going to tell my granddaddy." These words sent a shockwave through the teenagers' bodies, and they quickly convinced me that if I told anyone I would get in trouble and everyone would know that I was a "faggot". I did not fully comprehend what the word "faggot" meant. In the 1980s, the word "faggot" was used in playing fighting or conversation, so I did not equate the word to any homosexual content or derogatory connotation as it is today. I just knew that being in trouble was something I did not want, and that was enough to silence me. As I think now, it's crazy to me, and definitely shows the immaturity of them to suggest that I would be labeled such a term, but they were innocent of the term even though they were the offenders.

The word "trouble" echoing in my ear, I left the house and went to my house for a snack. I remember my grandfather giving me an orange and asking me if I had been crying. I told him no and retreated back out the door, but strangely I went back to the house of my molestation. As I approached the porch, I could see the boys looking out of the blinds as though they expected trouble to be coming. One of them opened the door fearfully asking if I had told my grandfather what had happened. I assured them that I did not and offered them some of my orange, which they graciously accepted. I do not remember much more from that day. I know they did not harm me anymore. Maybe it was the guilt of their actions or the fact that I showed somewhat of an allegiance to them by not telling on them. Throughout my childhood, I never saw much of those teenagers. It's possible that I could have seen them many times in passing but couldn't recall their faces. The house of the offense and my former house ironically was torn down and built into a church. I have visited the church on several occasions as both a speaker and an attendee. The feeling of what took place on that property is always a chilling reminder to me. Walking into the church bathroom quickly becomes that bedroom in which I felt my innocence was debauched.

I know the question that probably is ringing in your head. Why did I go back to that house? Honestly, I think that the acts I had endured made me their friend. Remember, I stated that acceptance was important to me, and being so young, I did not have the discernment to even notice what I allowed was a despicable act. During my childhood there was not an Erin's Law or much education presented on being molested, especially being a boy. No school guidance counselor ever conducted a lesson on being inappropriately touched or made to do things that were harmful to you. I not only thought that these acts were appropriate for their friendship, but also going back to share my orange with them. Wow. Sharing my orange would eventually serve as a peace-offering to those that violated me. How many abused people are guilty of giving a peace-offering to their violators and not even realize it? I was in that moment more afraid to get them in trouble than to be vindicated for their crime against me. I wonder if at any point in their lives they saw that orange as a sign of my innocence or a little ray of forgiveness being offered from a child. I often think that maybe that orange served as a deterrent for those teenagers hurting other children. It may sound silly, but this is the hope that no other children have to endure the shame and humiliation I've experienced all of these years.

It is crazy just what the mind captures as it relates to details. The fact that only two faces I remember when there were four in all could be associated with one being the abuser and the other being what I felt would be the protector. The one I saw as a protector was someone that I felt knew better because his siblings were my age. Would he have signed off on his brothers being treated the same way? I often wonder if he would have allowed this vicious act to happen to people that he loved for the sake of being accepted by the cocky teenager. Moments like this should cause us to reflect on how many times we stand back aimlessly while someone is being abused verbally or physically and say nothing out of the fear of not being accepted. Needing help and not receiving it caused me to always stand up for those in need. From that moment, I learned never to be a bully and always be a friend. I was a protector and friend for all, but, where was my friend?

It's crazy to think that most men that suffered molestation see themselves as protectors, but not vulnerable enough to see protection. I realize now the deep wound that was placed in my heart when it came to seeking help in any respect. I never felt safe in discussing my insecurities or deep thoughts. I became what others needed me to be and truly lost myself in the process.

Chapter Three

Drowned By Perversion

According to the English Language, **cause and effect** is a relationship between events or things, where one is the result of the other or others, a combination of action and reaction. The change of events that followed that day will be shocking to most people, however, those that stuffed the effects of sexual abuse will understand many of these events. The biggest myth that surrounds the subject of boys being molested by the same sex is that the boys will develop homosexual tendencies. Many men that have been molested shared with me that after they were molested a deep perversion for women sat in and a distaste for anything relating to homosexuality immersed within them.

I can relate to this situation because after that experience a deep level of perversion came over me so strongly. Now, I understand from about 6 years old to around 11 years old was pretty much normal. I was able to isolate that particular issue out of my life by simply not thinking about it. Over that period of time the faces got fuzzy and the names were forgotten. However, the seed of perversion would soon be ignited. This time the seed would not be molestation, but pornography.

For some reason, in the early 1990s, "sex" was a hot topic and popular world. Even though I was in my early adolescent years, I couldn't help hearing the greatest of having sex from my peers. Even though they were all lying back then to appease the other, I was very engulfed in the conversation. How do I know they were lying? Well, because I was lying about my experiences with girls as well. Thinking about it now, I had some of the worst lies imaginable, but I must say they were creative. My fuel for lust was also enhanced by my best friend's unlimited access to his father's pornographic videotape collection. We could literally go into his parents' room and watch all of the porn we wanted without fear of being disciplined. I remember the first tape vividly and the fear that came over me when his dad came down the hall. I knew that getting caught would lead to exposure, and my having spiritual parents, this situation was not going to go over well. However, this would not be the case as his father simply looked at what we were watching, changed his shoes, and left the room. Pure shock consumed my body, but my friend never reacted to his father coming into the room. From that point on, we watched porn as though we were watching cartoons. According to *A Man's Life, Featured, Porn Addiction*, "Porn is a substitute for actual sex, but our brain doesn't know that." When encountering sexual images, the brain is going to ramp up dopamine levels. These dopamines serve as the reward given to the body for survival". To make it simpler, the more pornographic material a person consumes, the more the body becomes dependent on that substance for survival.

What I realized was that I was going down a road that would haunt me for years. I had been molested,which exposed me to sexual acts early, and at 12 years old overconsuming myself in pornographic material. One door was opening the door to another door, and I had no control to stop it. On one hand, I was escaping the homosexual acts that plagued my mind, and on the other hand, I was creating a world of perversion that presented meaningless fantasies. These fantasies, as harmless as people make them out to be, actually caused an interference in how I saw women. For example, a normal child can go to school and perceive the female educator in the purest sense, however for me the opportunity for that educator to entertain the notion of sleeping with me after class was my fantasy. I did not understand that my purity was slowly becoming a monster that was hard to tame. The mere fact that I wanted sexual contact so early was constantly being fueled by friends talking about it all the time. Even though I was still a virgin physically, my mind was entering into worlds that were fitting for someone with sexual experience.

The mere fact that I had so many pornographic scenes in my mind was insane. It was like I could recall each scene no matter how long it had been since I saw it. A lot of people that haven't dealt with pornography are not aware of how powerful it is. I compare it to a drug addiction in how it can make you crave it. I didn't realize that I was fighting a battle on multiple fronts at such a young age. The open door that I was walking into was full of perversion. I was so full of fantasy that pornographic material proved that my reality was tainted.

So at twelve years old, every adolescent is supposed to get that wonderful, enlightening talk about sex. For most males, this talk involves the changing of the body, why certain parts are enticed with lust and the consequences that come with pre-marital sex. Seemingly, this was not the case with my father, as his inordinate, electrifying speech was only "son don't have sex". Wait a minute, the man that I patterned myself after, from music to style, to the smoothing of my voice for the ladies, only told me not to have sex? In all regards, my first real "man talk" should have been more thought-provoking and explosive. At least it should have been on the lines of all the lies that my friends were telling me or at least in comparison to the pornographic details I had witnessed. The lies of my friends coupled with a great sense of lust were more empowering than the words of my father.

At twelve years old, my parents had no idea of what I experienced at six years old. It was not a case of trust, but honestly, I did not think about the incident much. I did not know that one thing was connected to the other, and so I just did my best to delete the incident from my mind. We were in church strongly and so the issue of molestation never was a topic of discussion. Even in my school, being touched by an adult was a common theme, but being wrongly touched by another child/ teenager was not talked about. The issue of homosexuality was not a topic of discussion either, in fact, all I know was how disgusting and nasty it was. It needs to be understood that a lot of knowledge and topics talked about today were not popular topics during the late 80s, early 90s. With the changing of the world came different focuses; gangster rap had replaced Michael Jackson, Prince, and Luther Vandross, movies were becoming more graphic with love scenes, drugs, and police brutality; those were the hot topics of the day. Not to mention, being raised in a spiritual house did not give much lead to topics outside of the church. I also need for you to understand that my mother, as holy as she was, was and is still pretty ruthless when it comes to her kids. Not only would she have gotten angry at the boys, but would have tracked them down and went to jail for her actions. My stepfather and biological father are not good with bad information either; so unless I wanted to be an orphan, it was better to conceal the truth. So, rather than say anything I simply acted as if nothing had happened. Remember I'm still under the word "trouble", but now "trouble" is not wanting to see those I love get into "trouble".

According to the training for the Oakdale Police Department on "*Molestation: The Indicators*", it suggested that some of the main indicators of victims of molestation are bedwetting, drawings or writings of sexual theme subjects, outbursts of crying, abusing drugs, and/or attempts to run away from home. I'm sure that many studies and data was used to conclude these indicators, however, many boys have been molested and show none of these indicators. In fact, many operate as upstanding citizens, fathers, church leaders, and men in general. I did notice that the majority of men I interviewed for this portion of the book had one thing in common and that was the usage of pornographic material. In asking them why was pornographic material such a need, there was a resounding response that the fantasies displayed were more powerful than the actual act of intercourse. One man stated: "Pornography is a drug within itself, because once addicted the need grows stronger." He was molested by an uncle who further vitiated his youth by indulging him in pornographic material.

On two occasions I was caught with pornographic material, the first as a teenager and the second as a newly married adult. As a teenager, my parents focused on the abomination of the material and how it would disrupt moral consciousness. Even though having them approach the topic from a spiritual position did not ease the desire to partake in the material. Maybe if I had revealed my secret to them it would have been a different conversation, but at the time it was still a part of my life I did not want to reveal.

I want to take a brief moment to explain what happens when those closest to us are not aware of our struggle. The reasoning I gave my parents for the pornographic material was a surface-level answer, I told them I want to understand how to please my future spouse. What a dumb response! But at that time it worked, because it was the first issue on that level that my parents had to deal with. My mother was totally grossed out by the whole ordeal and my stepfather wanted to seem cool but knew if it was serious with my mom, he at least had to play the hard role. The discussion worked for that instance, but anyone that has ever dealt with any addiction on any level knows that the issue will go away, but the temptation will always be there.

Ten years later, the pornographic material would resurface in my life. Two years into my marriage and five years after accepting the call into ministry, I found myself revisited by the temptation. A friend of mine sent me an article digitally that wasn't graphic, but the woman in the story was a former porn star. The curiosity to research the star was overwhelming, and I found myself glued to the computer screen. Once or twice a week for about two months, I found myself interested in the vast storylines created.

Those two months were the hardest for me because of my relationship with the Lord. Okay, so I know there will be some of you that will ask: "What about your relationship with your wife?" Let me explain it this way. People who are addicted to pornography rarely consider the hurt it may cause to their spouse or the person they are in a relationship with because it seems innocent to that person. Consider other addictions and how the addicted person can't see the hurt being inflicted on those around them. In talking with people that have struggled with drug addiction, they never considered how their addiction was hurting their family members. To them, it was about getting a high or quick fix, and that's the same way pornography presents itself for those addicted to it. So, at that moment the way my wife may perceive this addiction was not apparent to me.

One night, my wife was preparing our baby son for a bath, and I was in the computer room watching some pornographic videos. I had the headset on so that the sounds would not draw the suspicion of my wife. Unbeknownst to me, she was calling me to participate in bathing our son. When she did not hear a response from me, she entered the computer room at such a speed that it did not give me time to click out of the material. The look on her face was not one of disgust, but one of disappointment. When asked why I was on the site, my response was simply: "I want to spice up our marriage". Months later, I would learn from my wife that pornography can create a feeling of low self-esteem in a spouse. The recklessness of my act created a hole in the heart of the one I vowed to honor and respect. Instead of taking that moment to come clean concerning the addiction, and what happened to me as a child. I went into "hidden secret cover-up" and apologized for the act. Even though forgiveness was granted, the healing that I needed to overcome was not established. I would continue on a path of hurt until that moment when the mask came off. Unfortunately, it would be many years before I would reveal the secret that haunted me for years. Remember "hurt people, hurt people!"

Chapter Four

Hiding In The Church

Some people will call a Christian fake for not overcoming all of their issues at once. Our society often depicts the "Haves from the Have Nots", you are either all the way saved (with no issues) or someone on the fence. So, the fear of telling my parents was one fear, but the fear of being exposed to the church was a whole different monster. My mother really got involved in church when she met my stepfather. Guess where they met? Yes. In church.

With mom being sold out for the Lord and my stepfather being a musician, most of our time was dedicated to the church. I grew accustomed to the church atmosphere, it was the one place that I felt the most comfortable. I was in the choir and even though I could not sing, no one in church criticized me (not to my face at least). I could not dance either, but dancing was encouraged and so I danced. I was not the most handsome young man, but the church girls found me attractive (most likely because not a lot of young guys were at our church). The church for me was my escape from the realities of being bullied in school, not being popular, not being celebrated by teachers, and the drama that came with being a kid. By the age of 14, I was one of the most popular kids in my church. I had the showmanship of a quartet singer and biblical knowledge that separated me from the other kids. Not to mention, I was often rewarded publicly by preachers that gave me an added advantage with church girls. Everything that I was not getting from outside of the church, I was definitely getting from inside the church including---sexual experiences.

I realized that being molested could do so much to a person. The longing to feel accepted was used against me when I was molested, and my continuing to want to be their friend after the act led me on a path of seeking acceptance from people. Even at the risk of losing myself or going against what was right, I had to have that acceptance in order to feel good about myself. I was longing for something that was stripped away from me and did not realize how broken I was. I was not longing for love, but longing for acceptance, and the person that was seeking it was not me, but the six-year-old boy inside me. The more biblical understanding I gained, the more I was in a fight with the inner man. On one hand, I knew that with faith I could overcome all things, but I also knew that my past was a hindrance to my growth. I was so afraid of dealing with the humiliation of my past that I suppressed it with the workings of the church. Do you know how many people are hiding their issues, because of the ugliness of their past? How about those operating in the church with secrets so scary they have to conceal them from others?

I did not see my life as being fake. I honestly saw my life as adapting to an ugly situation. In the church, I did not have to deal with the past. In most cases, I was encouraged to forget the stigma of the past and live according to the present. I was being taught in the church that forgetting was the act of never thinking about a situation, as though God would magically take the thought from my mind, and I would never be haunted by it again. People who do not understand the trauma often think that a person can just forget (absence of thought). The reality is trauma is a life-long process that has to be worked out before a person can move forward from it. Even in our best attempts to fake our way through life, real trauma will constantly seek us out and eventually expose us to the world. The National Center for Biotechnology Information (NCBI) writes, *"The impact of trauma can be subtle, insidious, or outright destructive. How an event affects an individual depends on many factors, including characteristics of the individual, the type and characteristics of the event(s), developmental processes, the meaning of the trauma, and sociocultural factors."*

In short, most males that have dealt with trauma from molestation or sexual abuse have not been taught or counseled on how to deal with the effects of the action/actions, so you cannot tell them to forget it (absence of thought). However, there is a scripture that I used that taught me the correct way to forgive and forget.

My scripture for moving forward was Philippians 3:13: **"Brothers and sisters, I do not consider myself yet to have taken hold of it. But one thing I do: Forgetting what is behind and straining toward what is ahead."** To me forgetting was the absence of remembrance, nonetheless, what I learned later was that forgetting is the benefit of moving forward. So many times we want to forget (absence of remembering), but that will never be possible. We have to learn the benefits of moving forward so that when reminded of the incident, we have the victory over it. I learned the power was in seeing the benefits of me moving forward. Yes, what happened to me was ugly, but I was not going to allow an ugly event to destroy me. The straining towards what is ahead in the scripture was me basically saying, "No matter what it cost, I was determined to win." To every person of trauma reading this, understanding your confession to move forward is vital to your survival.

More topics of discussion need to be had in church to help foster the deliverance of so many that are bound by their past. So many churchgoers are fighting secret battles that they feel will bring humiliation and contempt if they are exposed. These people hide behind titles, church positions, and in pews afraid of really going beneath the surface to break free from their hurtful experiences. I remember being told, "Fake it to you make it". This concept is basically acting like it is alright even if it is not. I think this phrase has value in the concept of not letting everyone know your problems, so you fake it to make it. However, in any other cases, this statement hides the very truth to your deliverance and healing. Instead of having to fake anything, I want you to read this book and be able to confront your past head-on.

Chapter Five

The Process Of Forgiveness

Twenty-seven years had passed, I never considered the thought of forgiveness. Instead I just suppressed the pain. I just wrote my first book, *Learn to Take Back Your Mind*, and I remember sitting on a television show being interviewed. The interviewer was asking all kinds of questions about how we take back our minds. Not to sound braggadocios, but I was killing the interview. I knew all the right words to say and then he asked a question about forgiveness. Like any good writer, I was thinking of forgiveness from a spiritual perspective, and without thinking I answered it according to how I would answer as a preacher. The more I began to dive into forgiveness the more he started asking me personal questions about how I got to the point of forgiving my molesters. At 33 years old, I'm now in my teaching profession.

I'm doing the things that I always wanted to do in my life. I'm married and have three children. The concept of forgiveness was never really an issue for me or so I thought. The interviewer's questions stayed in my mind long after he asked the question. I felt like I had given him a fake answer. It was at that moment that I realized my whole approach to the situation was more of a cover-up than a victory.

There are times in our lives where we feel like we're done with a situation based on the fact that we just don't remember it or we really don't think about it. Have we forgiven the issue? This was going to be very important for me moving forward with my life. That question made me realize that even though the offense happened 27 years prior, I still had not forgiven the situation. I'll be honest and say that I overlooked it. I didn't think about it. Or basically, I just didn't care to allow it to be in my mind. But I know that I did not forgive the situation.

Now I have to admit the mistakes of my preaching made forgiveness seem very easy. To just bottle up all of your hurt and pain, all of your suffering, and crying and in one magic moment just let it all go out and forgive. Ha! What a joke! I mean you have to realize that not only did these boys not seek my forgiveness, but I could only remember two of them. Then you have to account for the fact that it happened so long ago. How do you walk up to full-grown men and tell them what they did to you?

Can you imagine the humiliation and embarrassment that would come from their denial? It's basically telling a young man that somewhere in his teenage years he wrestled with homosexual thoughts. Oh yeah, that's going to go over well being that this person could now be married with children. So rather than thinking of forgiveness, I thought to just move on from the situation.

I was listening to a sermon by Dr. Norma Gray and she said, "It is a difference between moving on and moving forward." She explained that moving on was just a process of moving horizontally from one situation to another situation, however moving forward was actually dealing with the issue so that the future is brighter. For 27 years, I have moved on, but I have not moved forward. In my mind I moved on in the way that I dealt with the memory of the molestation, but I never really moved forward from the situation. You can always tell when you move forward from a situation because that situation becomes the story you use to encourage someone else. True forgiveness is not just saying I accept the apology, but true forgiveness is I can take the hurt and pain that was done to me, and I can use it to promote who God is in my life.

To say that this would be an easy task is just like saying that it is easy for the cow to jump over the moon. Honestly, forgiveness is probably easily obtainable when the person that offends you comes to you seeking forgiveness. Even in an extreme situation hearing the words

"I'm sorry" or "Please forgive me" brings a small step of direction for full forgiveness. So how do you forgive someone without an apology? Well, the first thing I had to understand was that the forgiveness I was trying to obtain was not going to come from my carnal mindset. In fact, it is very difficult for a person to think that they can forgive without some sort of divine intervention. I was reminded of when Jesus was on the cross and he said, "Father forgive them for they know not what they do." I had to liken that to the teenagers that molested me. In their young, immature minds they actually did not know what they were doing. I also came to realize that for my story to be complete I had to endure the pain of the past. Without the crushing of grapes, we have no wine, and as our lives are crushed it produces the oil of our anointing. I used Romans 8:28, *"And we know that all that happens to us is working for our good if we love God and are fitting into his plans,"* as my guide through the forgiving process. I came to understand that this scripture doesn't mean everything in life will be good, but with purpose, it works for our good in the end. Now you are probably asking how a situation like that work for my good.

To that question, I would simply say that this situation gave me a story that I could share with others in a similar situation. A story that not many males are willing to share, but so many are suffering from the negative effects of child molestation. Even though I had to go through some humiliating times of shame and guilt, it was that story that can help someone today.

How can you forgive someone without an apology? Now, I have to be honest with you. It's easier to forgive someone that acknowledges wrongdoing faster than it is to forgive someone who has not apologized to you. The answer simply lies within you and how much time you have to waste on being angry and upset. It took me over 20 years to see how this humiliated moment in my life was going to work for my good. I've heard it said many times that forgiveness is for the individual and not for the one that hurt them, but oftentimes we allow ourselves, through our unforgiveness, to create a prison that we didn't deserve to be in. For all of those years, I found myself being sentenced to an offense that I could not help, that I could not prevent, and could not forget. The longer I allowed myself to walk in unforgiveness, the longer my healing was being delayed. Yes, I'll be the first to admit that healing is a process that takes forgiveness to be effective. The longer you give your offender the power over you, the longer you suffer in life. The healing that I am describing cannot come from the apology of an offender, and so many times we feel that we need that in order to heal.

True freedom is released inwardly before it shows up outwardly. Many people want to look free even though mentally they are bound. I wanted inward healing so that I could face the situation without shame or guilt. In other words, to be able to go forth in your life without having to be dependent on an apology is more freeing than actually getting an apology within itself. Let me clear this up for you. An apology is good if you got it, but if you haven't, do not wait to get one. Simply live free so your dependency is not on the person that molested you.

Forgiveness is about the person that was offended taking back the power from their offender. When I forgave those boys for the negative impact they had on my life, I took back my power from the stigma of the situation. I could no longer give my peace to them, nor could I continue to be haunted by the past. To be fully transparent with you, my forgiveness allowed me to have empathy for my offenders. Even though they were young and immature, I felt bad for them and their actions. I believe I connected with Jesus on the cross when he looked at his mockers and stated, "Father, forgive them for they know not what they do." You may not be at that point of empathy and you may never get to that place, but you must learn the true power of forgiveness so you can be free.

Chapter Six

The Process Of Healing

Transparency: *implies openness, communication, and accountability* (Webster's Dictionary). There has to be a place of transparency within yourself that you feel the freedom to express what happened to you. Many people are afraid to go into those narratives because they are afraid of what they're going to uncover, such as feelings of anguish, pain, hurt, anxiety, or shame. Rather than dealing with those situations, they just bottle them up and try to forget them. Transparency can be the hardest part of the process because recounting or retailing the story will be a moment of real freedom and torture at the same time. I remember the moment when I was living in my truth. I had so much fear come over me that I was stuttering in my delivery. I did not know how transparent to be or how much to tell, but the more I let it out, the better I started to feel.

Now I'm not telling you to be transparent as far as telling everybody in the world. Everyone needs that one person they can trust to be naked (transparent) in front of them who will not judge them for not being perfect. I believe that it is at the transparency stage that the majority of people are fighting the most, because this is really the moment of truth. And even though we say we want the truth, in reality we hide the truth from ourselves because the truth can be ugly. At that moment in my life, I've probably cried more tears than I had ever cried in my life. I slowly began to feel the weights being lifted off of my shoulders. I want to tell you the freedom that I felt from that day was unbelievable.

It's crazy how long and how much weight we allow ourselves to carry from our past. I allowed that 6-year-old boy to finally have his moment where he could speak. I had suppressed his tears for so long. I silenced him and told him not to be real. I flooded him with so much perversion and fantasies that I had continued the assault on his innocence. I continued to open up his wounds and even though I did not start it, I continued the abuse. At that moment, I had to allow the six year old to breathe, speak, cry, and to be free. This in turn freed the 33-year-old man from his bondage and fake life!

Now I want you to understand that within the transparency stage you're also breaking free from the fear that the moment cost you. Most people are afraid to be transparent because they fear the backlash that's going to come from them telling their truth. This fear makes them go into a cocoon within their mind; they attempt to operate in freedom, but they are bound mentally. Being free from fear does not mean you won't cringe at the thought of the offense. Even in writing this book, I often cringed at the reality I faced at six years old. Understanding that total deliverance does not come without aftershocks is very important to transparency. I believe it is this cringing sensation that makes us human and able to operate from a real place. So removing the thought that total deliverance is being free from the cringing is not absolutely necessary or real.

Before I could get to the place of comfort in telling my story, I started out with small transparency. In order words, I told my experience to people that I could trust to pray for me and uplift me. In a "social media age" there is always the temptation to make false, bold declarations. In order to divert from healing, many people post false claims of well-being and mediocre transparency. These false claims lead the audience to believe that the individual is good and creates a wall of deception for the victim. The small steps of transparency have to be removed from a public audience. As Bishop Rudolph McKissick Jr. stated in one of his sermons, "Never give a majority platform to minority people."

Before I could go public with my truth, I shared it in private with those who could help me build the truth into a testimony. Rushing the transparency step could lead to hurt feelings because everyone cannot comprehend the experience. Think about some of the people that came out against celebrities in situations of rape and molestation, or those that confronted the family by revealing the family secret. Outsiders to the struggle could not comprehend how deep the person's hurt was. They have empathy for the individual as they try to process the hurt of someone else. They feel as though soothing words and a hug will suffice. When establishing transparency with your chosen small group or confidant, confirm that they provide a safe place to return to as you go through the process. I found myself constantly crying and sharing until I was able to move forward in the transparency state.

The transparency process is not the completion. It merely allows you to come to grips that the offense derailed the normal flow of your person. Transparency is allowing others to see your unabbreviated honesty. It invites others into the fullness of who you are without rehearsal or putting on a stage production. It holds others accountable to either your healing or their breakthrough. It does not seek approval from others, but it allows the person to walk in their full truth. It requires a person to be vulnerable, which can be very scary. Transparency has to be coupled with bravery.

Bravery: *the quality or state of having or showing mental or moral strength in the face of danger, fear, or difficulty.* (Webster's Dictionary) The bravery to move forward was one of the hardest things to do. It takes a big leap of faith to step into the unknown. For many victims of molestation, the bravery is to tell the story, heal, love, or even embrace the reality that it isn't their fault. It is easy to try to forget a situation, but with bravery, a person can look their trauma in the eye and decree victory over it. I did not understand at the start of healing how much courage I would need to finish the process.

The very act of putting myself in front of the critics and the naysayers was a terrifying experience. How was I going to tell my parents, my wife, my church, and my family the secret that I successfully held onto for so many years? I was so afraid of breaking the balance of my reality, destroying the life that operated without anyone knowing of what I faced at six years old. So, much of my success was being able to ignore this tragedy. I considered everyone's feelings very carefully. I knew the pain it would cause my parents and the feelings of mistrust it would cause my wife. I also knew the backlash it would create from those that think men and women use trauma as an excuse not to accept responsibility for their negative actions. As I considered these thoughts, the Lord reminded me of those that needed someone to be upfront and honest for the sake of seeing others delivered. That was the moment when bravery kicked in and reminded me that a "yes" to the Lord is not always an easy road, but it is a road worth traveling.

On the road to healing, I had to come to the point of wanting the healing more than the hurt. For so many years, I hid the hurt to function in the world, however not dealing with the hurt halted the healing process. When you avoid dealing with an issue doesn't make the issue magically disappear, it only holds the issue to the side until a trigger causes the issue to resurface. The issue can resurface in doubt, depression, anxiety, a womanizing nature, pornography, broken relationships, mistrust, or divorce. The biggest hindrance to the healing for me was avoidance. If you are in the avoidance phase of your life, please know that the hurt will forever be with you until you successfully deal with it. Do you have the courage to face the hurt head-on in order to succeed? About five years ago, our church had a motto: "Winning is the Only Option." This motto was our way of looking at life and motivating ourselves to win. When dealing with molestation, you have to develop a "Winning is the Only Option" mindset. No successful fight comes without opposition.

The book of Samuel in *The Bible* talks about a shepherd boy named David. Even though the Prophet Samuel spoke a kingdom over David when he was a young boy, it wasn't until David defeated Goliath, survived betrayal, and overcame countless enemies that his success was within reach. Goliath posed a great challenge to David, he was bigger in stature, more experienced, and feared amongst all men. Your hurt may seem like a Goliath in your life, but here is a news flash, your hurt has hurt more than just you! You are not the only person that has been molested or sexually assaulted, so this hurt is bigger and more experienced than you. In the story, King Saul offered David his armor, but David refused because he knew he had to use his skills and not someone else's armor. Your Goliath will not be defeated with someone else's armor, but the bravery on the inside of you will show you how to use your weapons.

David's greatest challenge was not his Goliath but the betrayal of someone he loved. In most molestation cases, the molester is a close family member or friend of the family; According to the 1in6 website, 90% of children molested know their offenders compared to 10% molested by strangers. David loved King Saul, but due to jealousy, Saul didn't return the same sentiments. Betrayal can only really come from someone with access to your heart. In talking with different men who share my experience, a close, trusted family member betrayed most of them.

Molestation is a two-fold situation because it causes severe damage and trust is severely impacted as well. This lack of trust can be displaced in relationships, friendships, and even faith in a deity. David's betrayal was something that he could not stop. Molestation was something that I could not stop, but the bravery to allow God to help me was my choice.

David had multiple enemies he had to overcome on his way to his palace. People who have never experienced molestation have no clue of the other enemies that tag along with it. Not only are you dealing with the act of molestation, but here comes shame, guilt, embarrassment/ humiliation, trust issues, identity crisis, and many other emotions and fears. Bravery is not displaced where there is no great threat. Heroes aren't produced where there is no challenge to overcome. As David defeated his enemies his threats to his kingdom were being diminished. As you deal with molestation and the other enemies that come along with it, the threats to your happiness will slowly diminish and real freedom will be long-lasting.

Support: *bear all or part of the weight of; to give assistance to.* (Webster's Dictionary) Even if you are a boy or man of faith, having support is allowing someone to help you shoulder the burden of the effects of molestation.

Don't be like I was. I allowed the humiliation and the secrecy to hinder the healing process. I had a great support system around me from my immediate family, my church family, and eventually my marriage, however, I was stuck in the stage of avoidance where I didn't cry out for help. I was afraid that I was going to either be judged or the hurt would be mitigated to an excuse.

People that have never experienced this kind of trauma may not understand why a person would not cry out. For a lot of people, it's hard to fathom a person carrying so much hurt and pain around for so many years. In reality, everyone has an unbearable secret hiding in the shadows. Just like a person may carry around their ugly secret, so do victims of molestation, especially men. Understand men aren't necessarily equipped for how to handle mental or emotional pain. For example, when a man is hurt he is told to get back up, and he better not cry. So, most men grow up with a numbness towards pain. A strong support system helps with openness and complete transparency. It allows the man to see that he has the right to cry or express himself in non-judgmental ways. The more support I felt, the more I healed properly. I didn't realize how much of a release it was to talk to someone that loved me considering the past. It gave me the strength I needed to minister from this platform I have today.

Research has shown that a strong support system has many benefits, including longer life expectancy, less stress, and reduced depression and anxiety. I remember as a teenager battling low self-esteem and depression. At the time, I didn't evaluate these feelings of molestation; I just thought it was a teenage identity thing. After a pity argument with my aunt and grandmother, I went into the medicine cabinet and swallowed nine of my grandmother's pills. Before I attempted this suicidal act, I called my then-girlfriend to tell her what I was about to do. I hung up before she could talk me out of it. This would be the first time I attempted to commit suicide, but it wouldn't be the last. Each attempt was a call to be loved, rather than trying to end my life. If this is a "what moment" for you, I suggest you go back to Chapter 2 when I talked about the orange and the need to feel loved.

Where there is a lack of information, the mind is led to fantasy. The truth is that we have more support than we realize. The mind without factual information will lead us down a tunnel where we feel alone, isolated, or like we are the only ones that have experienced trauma even though others have as well. Don't allow yourself to struggle in secret and put on a fake smile for the public. Talk to people that can minister to you, encourage you, counsel you, and if need be, cry with you. I wish that I had allowed my parents to support me through those years of struggle. When I finally told them, I was already grown and established in my own family. Even within my own family, I still left my wife in the dark out of shame and guilt. I want to minister this to your spirit, avoid letting shame and guilt box you in where you will not allow people who love you to help you.

Chapter Seven

Do You Want To Be Made Whole

One of my favorite stories in *The Bible* lies in the Book of John, the fifth chapter. The setting of the story is near the pool called Bethesda near the Sheep's Gate in Jerusalem. The author, John, tells us that this pool was surrounded by the invalids---blind, lame, and paralyzed. In the earliest manuscripts, there is no explanation for why these invalids were there, but later scholars added an explanation that can be found in the fourth verse. According to the text, people believed that an angel of the Lord would come down from heaven and stir the waters. Whoever was the first to enter the pool after the waters were stirred would be healed of his infirmities.

When Jesus sees a man who has been ill for 38 years lying by the pool, he asks the man, "Do you want to be made whole?" Instead of shouting a resounding "Yes!" The man offers Jesus a complaint about how there is no one to put him into the pool. We can conclude that the man has been in the situation so long that being made whole would only be accomplished with the help of someone else. I wish I could tell you that after being hurt by molestation someone would magically be able to put you in a magical pool of deliverance. The fact that the man's response was to say no one was there to put him in the water is a sermon within itself.

We may want others to do the hard work for us and help us get to the place of being able to live free of the pain. However, this life that we are living rarely comes with a Lifetime or Hallmark ending. I remember wanting my parents to see my hurt and guide me to the point of releasing my secret. I remember hoping my wife would see my immaturity and help me release my secret so that she could understand my inner hurt. What about all of those preachers and church folks that could hear from the Lord? They were so quick to tell me what the Lord wanted from my life, but not one could see the hurt I was masking. I can admit that I was waiting on someone to help me get into the pool. I want to minister this to your spirit, avoid letting shame and guilt box you in where you will not allow people who love you to help you.

I always wonder how the man got to the pool. Did he crawl? Did someone drop him off at the pool? When he got there obviously something hindered his progression to the pool. How many attempts have you made to be free from the hurt, but something blocked your progression? I can remember several times I was close to sharing the details of my past, but the fear overpowered my tongue, and I stayed silent. The hardest part of being made whole is finding the strength to want deliverance. In the text, the man says he gets to the pool, but others beat him to the water. So, he had just enough faith to get to the water, but not enough to get in the water. I hope you get the courage to get into the water from reading this book.

Jesus responds to the man's complaint by telling him to stand up, take up his mat, and walk. Immediately the man is healed and takes up his mat and walks. Oftentimes in telling this story, I imagine the mat symbolizing a comfortable place of hurt, excuses, and stagnation. The wholeness you need to combat molestation will never be accomplished as long as there is a comfortable bed of excuses to lay on. In order to be made whole the very excuses to stop progression have to be put aside. Instead of wishing the hurt away, you have to have a determination to be made whole. No one has to be more determined for your freedom than you. So when Jesus comes to you for wholeness, be prepared to pick up your excuses (mat) and walk away healed.

I hope this book encourages you with the desire to be made whole. It took a lot of strength and prayer to produce this work. A part of my wholeness was having the courage to complete the story that I kept hidden for so many years. Thirty-five years since the moment my life changed, I have grown as a husband, father, pastor, teacher, motivational speaker, and author. Even though this sounds strange, I credit that life-changing moment as a vital piece to my success. Even though the molestation was an ugly part of my history, without it, I probably wouldn't be the man I am today. Yes, I was molested! Yes, I had to battle with low self-esteem and depression! And yes, I fell into a tunnel of perversion and pornography! But, I'm thankful my story didn't end with those chapters, but turning the page of life allowed the ending to be better than the beginning. Boys are molested too. Maybe now the conversion will grow, and more men will be healed and delivered.

Testimonials

"I never considered my first sexual encounter to be abuse until I was in therapy for other issues. My therapist was helping me deal with some debilitating anxiety and depression and was reaching far back in the annals of my history in order to deal with those scars. She said something to me that triggered me regarding my childhood and it was at that moment I realized I had been molested. I was 5, and my mother cleaned houses for an affluent family in my community. At times, they would hire my mother to watch their children overnight as they went on trips. This one particular evening, the son came into my bedroom and began to fondle me. At five, you don't know how to deal with conflicting feelings of shame and pleasure so I pretended to be asleep and allowed it to happen. This took place each time I spent the evening at this home. I tucked it away into the recesses of my physique, not realizing its impact on my life was not buried, only hiding to show up later."— Attorney

"I wrestled with nightmares for the majority of my life. My wife wasn't aware of the struggles I dealt with in my past and I was afraid to share. My fear came from hearing those words spoken by my uncle, "If you tell anyone, they won't believe you." So I kept the struggle inside of myself for many years.

I was inappropriately touched from eight years old until I was twelve years old by my uncle and an older cousin.

My uncle didn't know that my cousin (his son) was touching me, but I'm sure my cousin was a victim of his dad's twisted thinking. How else could a son mimic the patterns of his father so accurately? Both started the molestation as just harmless and disguised it as playing. As the "playing" increased and got uncomfortable, both my uncle and cousin got fearful of their exposure and turned their deeds into my insecurity. They made me feel as though I allowed it and that telling on them was really me telling on myself. The events of what they did to me caused me many insecurities in life. It was very hard for me to trust anyone, including my wife. Even though I love her, there would be times during intimacy that I would room out of the room in fear. Molestation is more than a physical touch, it's an endless cycle of mental trauma."--- Preacher

"My first sexual experience came at the age of eight years old. Being raised in a single parent house, my mother would often leave me and my siblings with a babysitter. In the early 1970s, a babysitter was usually a neighborhood girl seeking some extra money. The babysitter on this one occasion was a young lady around 16 years old. She lived down the street from us and for the most part she never showed any interest in me or any boy to my knowledge.

One night, my mother went out with one of her friends to a party. After playing for most of the night, our babysitter told us it was time for bed. As my siblings dozed off and me half asleep, I felt a hand over my mouth. I opened my eyes to find our babysitter standing over me in her panties and a t-shirt. She told me to be quiet and follow her into my mother's room. She told me to get in the bed and then she started to fondle me. She then proceeded to kiss me and touch my private area. I'm sure your imagination can infer what happened next. When the act was done, she told me to keep it a secret or both of us would get in trouble. Needless to say, because of my secrecy she would commit this act three more times.

When I finally got to the age of being able to tell my story, I was surprised at the reaction I got. Due to it being a female that molested me, I was treated as though it wasn't as serious. In fact, I was told that she was making a man out of me and I was lucky. I was also told that molestation can only come from men. The aftermath caused me to become a sex addict. It took me years to even entertain the notion of settling down with one lady. The marriage only lasted for a few years due to perversion and inability to remain committed. After years of counseling, I was able to face my demons and I'm remarried to a great woman."-- Educator

References

Hill, Gerald N., and Kathleen Hill. Nolo's Plain-English Law Dictionary. Berkeley, CA: Nolo, 2009. Print.

New King's James Version Bible, 2001, Romans 8:28

Rape, Abuse & Incest National Network RAINN / National Sexual Assault Hotline . United States, 2002. Web Archive. https://www.loc.gov/item/lcwaN0008005/.

Statistics from https://1in6.org/get-information/the-1-in-6-statistic/. 2021

"The Understudied Female Sexual Predator". *The Atlantic*. 2016. https://www.theatlantic.com/science/archive/2016/11/the-understudied-female-sexual-predator/503492/

Printed in the United States
by Baker & Taylor Publisher Services